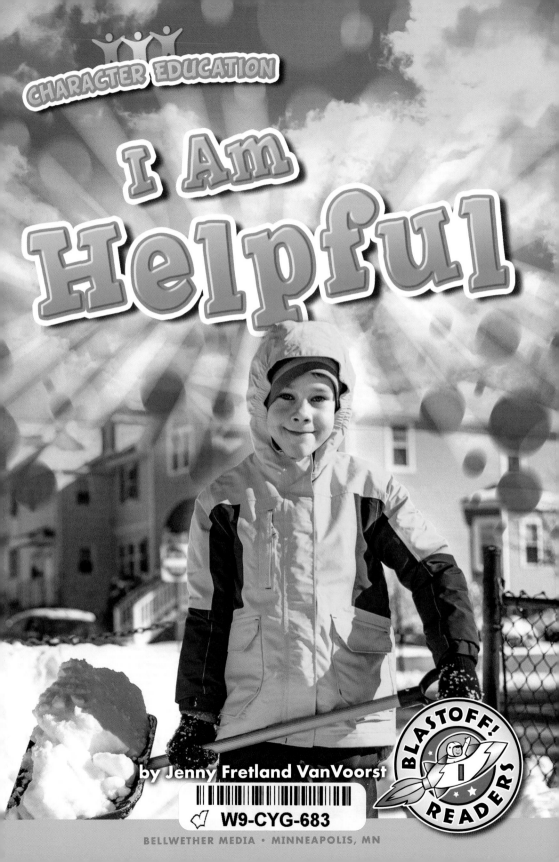

CHARACTER EDUCATION

I Am Helpful

by Jenny Fretland VanVoorst

W9-CYG-683

BELLWETHER MEDIA · MINNEAPOLIS, MN

Note to Librarians, Teachers, and Parents:

Blastoff! Readers are carefully developed by literacy experts and combine standards-based content with developmentally appropriate text.

Level 1 provides the most support through repetition of high-frequency words, light text, predictable sentence patterns, and strong visual support.

Level 2 offers early readers a bit more challenge through varied simple sentences, increased text load, and less repetition of high-frequency words.

Level 3 advances early-fluent readers toward fluency through increased text and concept load, less reliance on visuals, longer sentences, and more literary language.

Level 4 builds reading stamina by providing more text per page, increased use of punctuation, greater variation in sentence patterns, and increasingly challenging vocabulary.

Level 5 encourages children to move from "learning to read" to "reading to learn" by providing even more text, varied writing styles, and less familiar topics.

Whichever book is right for your reader, Blastoff! Readers are the perfect books to build confidence and encourage a love of reading that will last a lifetime!

This edition first published in 2019 by Bellwether Media, Inc.

No part of this publication may be reproduced in whole or in part without written permission of the publisher. For information regarding permission, write to Bellwether Media, Inc., Attention: Permissions Department, 6012 Blue Circle Drive, Minnetonka, MN 55343.

Library of Congress Cataloging-in-Publication Data

Names: Fretland VanVoorst, Jenny, 1972- author.
Title: I Am Helpful / by Jenny Fretland VanVoorst.
Description: Minneapolis, MN : Bellwether Media, Inc., [2019] |
   Series: Blastoff! Readers: Character Education | Audience: Age: 5-8. |
   Audience: K to Grade 3. | Includes bibliographical references and index.
Identifiers: LCCN 2018033413 (print) | LCCN 2018034865 (ebook) |
   ISBN 9781681036519 (ebook) | ISBN 9781626179264 (hardcover : alk. paper) |
   ISBN 9781618914972 (pbk. : alk. paper)
Subjects: LCSH: Helping behavior in children–Juvenile literature. | Children–Conduct of life–Juvenile literature.
Classification: LCC BF723.H45 (ebook) | LCC BF723.H45 F74 2019 (print) | DDC 179/.9–dc23
LC record available at https://lccn.loc.gov/2018033413

Text copyright © 2019 by Bellwether Media, Inc. BLASTOFF! READERS and associated logos are trademarks and/or registered trademarks of Bellwether Media, Inc. SCHOLASTIC, CHILDREN'S PRESS, and associated logos are trademarks and/or registered trademarks of Scholastic Inc., 557 Broadway, New York, NY 10012.

Editor: Christina Leaf   Designer: Jeffrey Kollock

Printed in the United States of America, North Mankato, MN

Table of Contents

What Is Helpfulness?

Your mom has a long **grocery list**. Wow! That is a lot of items.

Do you play on your phone? Or do you help her find things?

Helpful people do **useful** things for others. People may ask for help. You can **offer**, too.

Why Be Helpful?

Helpful people make life easier for others. This helps build **relationships**.

People feel good
when you help them.
You feel good, too!

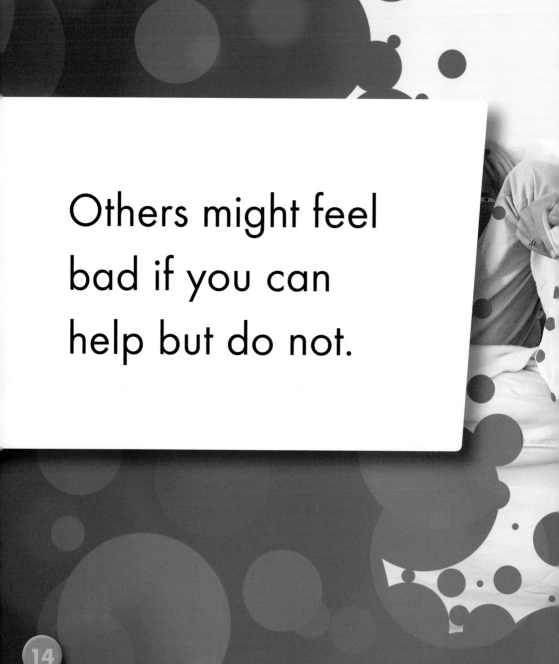

Others might feel
bad if you can
help but do not.

Who Is Helpful?

15

You Are Helpful!

There are many ways to be helpful. Help your grandma **rake** leaves.

Set the table for dinner.
Teach your brother
to tie his shoes.

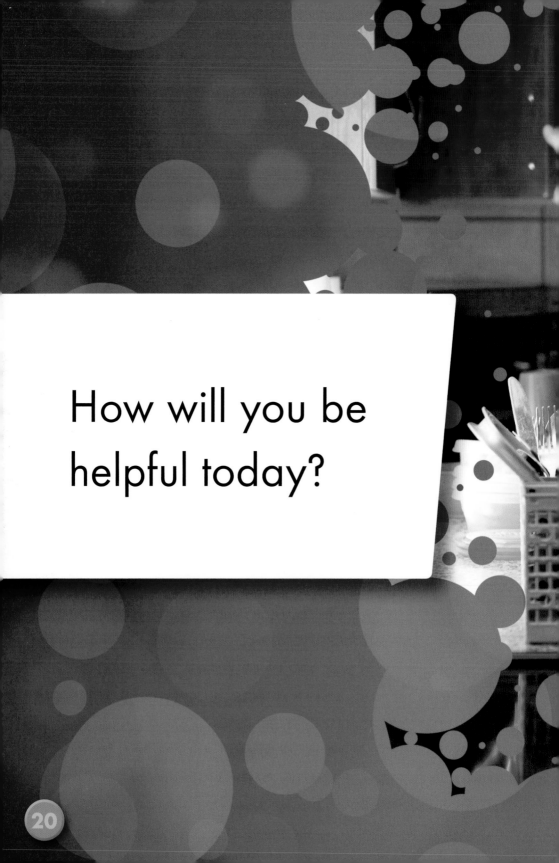

How will you be helpful today?

Glossary

grocery list

a list of food and other items to buy at a grocery store

relationships

ties with other people

offer

to make something open for use

useful

able to help do something

rake

to gather with a long-handled, forked garden tool

To Learn More

AT THE LIBRARY

Fortuna, Lois. *Helping a Friend*. New York, N.Y.: Gareth Stevens Publishing, 2016.

Nelson, Robin. *How Can I Help?: A Book About Caring*. Minneapolis, Minn.: Lerner Publications, 2014.

Ponto, Joanna. *Being Helpful*. New York, N.Y.: Enslow Publishing, 2016.

ON THE WEB

FACTSURFER

Factsurfer.com gives you a safe, fun way to find more information.

1. Go to www.factsurfer.com.

2. Enter "helpful" into the search box.

3. Click the "Surf" button and select your book cover to see a list of related web sites.

Index